MW01098642

MY MAUI

©1996 by My Island Publishing
P.O.Box 100
Volcano, Hi 96785
Ph. (808) 967-7216
Fax (808) 967-7719
E-mail: myisland@ilhawaii.net

ISBN - 1-885129-09-2

Cover design by Belknap Communications & Design
770 Kapiolani Blvd, Suite 604
Honolulu, Hi 96813

Printed by Publishers Express
Flambeau Litho Corporation
Ladysmith, Wi 54848

MY MAUI

CAN ALSO BE

YOUR MAUI

By Gordon Morse

All photographs by the author

Center spread painting and sketches by Joann Morse

CONTENTS

MY MAUI

LET'S BEGIN

The best way to remember a place much loved is to go back and find it no less than it was.

I hope this special tour booklet can help you experience Maui for the first time or refresh your memory on a revisit. Either way, I trust you will come to understand and love the island.

This writer has a 70 year-old relationship with The Valley Isle. I was raised in Maui County - on the island of Moloka'i to be exact - and Maui island was a youthful playground for me. I earned my Cub and Boy Scout merit badges here over half a century ago.

During adult working years my wife Joann and I owned a U-drive company in Kahului when today's brand of tourism was just beginning.

We built homes for the rich and famous on East Maui, and guest cottages for the first hotel in Kihei.

Almost 40 years ago, Joann was on the staff that researched and masterminded the process that eventually made Maui's port of Lahaina Hawaii's first historical district.

As a newsman for the State's major morning daily, I reported murders, fires, a tidal wave, yacht races, economic development, archeological finds, and covered the Maui County Fair in words and photos for more times than I care to remember.

An inquisitive group of us walked around Maui twenty-one years ago to discover what changes man and nature had made since the first tour book of this island was written in 1875.

In l996 Joann and I re-checked to see if we would find the Maui we love no less than it was for the purpose of writing this book.

The answer didn't surprise us. Maui is something old and new ---constantly being renewed --- at too fast a rate to suit some people. But in and around it all, plenty of the basic Maui we remembered was still there. That part is no less than it was.

Gordon Morse
Volcano, Hawaiii 1997

WHAT TO EXPECT HEREIN

Of all the Hawaiian islands, Maui has the most books written about its various assets: beaches, hiking, exploring, above and below water activities, volcanoes, flora and fauna, and history. These are well-documented, well-written and well-photographed works. (A partial list is available at the back of this booklet).

Gift shops offer racks of what is termed "throw away visitor literature" sponsored by the companies who advertise inside, with information catering to their commercial interests. There are also tourist guides sold nationwise that try to give it all, along with lists of every hotel, condo, car rental and restaurant.

This travel book attempts to do none of the above. Here you get a simple tour that tells it like it is. Along the way I touch on a little history and local color so what you see or experience may be more meaningful. If something is not worth your time or effort, I say so. When I have an educated opinion, or feel strongly about something, I will say that too, even if it gives a negative view of the island.

I have also correced a few misunderstandings and facts that have crept into popular literature, because some writers of the island scene simply copy what others have written and do not seek out original or updated souces of information.

We will not travel every road, as a trip to a place like Poli Poli Springs high on the south side of Haleakala is not attempted by the average visitor. The area should be experienced, but then Maui has to keep some secrets to itself.

The Maui map you will want to follow is by James A. Bier, published by the University of Hawaii. Available at most stores.

This is the Maui I know and love.

ARRIVAL

Today as I get off the jet at Kahului Airport, I have an entirely different first impression of Maui than in the past. Until recently, everyone was blown apart walking from the plane to a shed-like terminal parked several hundred feet away on the tarmac. The trade wind whipped across the runway and did a number on you. This cemented the idea that Maui was a windy island.

Not so today. I walk through a jetway from the plane into a new spacious terminal that seems to dwarf the runway. But just wait. A much longer runway to make Maui an international airport destination is coming.

Welcome to Maui No Ka Oe, which means, Maui is the best! Mauians must really think that, because"Maui" is printed, embossed, carved into, painted, and otherwise attached to almost everything you buy on this island.

WHAT'S IN A NAME

Some individual Hawaiian islands have been named three different times during the past 1,700 years. (It may have been four, but the first names have been lost forever, as nothing has passed down to us from the original Polynesian settlers who arrived around 300 A.D.) Sometime after that, other settlers and explorers gave the various islands the names we know now, although spelling and pronunciation differ today.

In the 1500s and early 1600s, the Spanish documented some of our islands on their Pacific-wide trading map. The group of islands was known as Los Majos. Hawaii island was called La Mesa due to the shape and flatish top of Mauna Loa. Maui was La Desgraciado or La Maja or Los Monjes (we aren't quite sure which because they simply grouped Maui, Moloka'i, Lana'i and Kaho'olawe together.) Other islands were given the names Rocca Partida and La Nublada. But the world didn't know that until the British captured one of their treasure galleons in 1743 and found their Pacific charts. For over 200 years they had kept their island discoveries and sailing routes secret.

When British Captain James Cook arrived in 1778, Maui was called Mowee, which he wrote down in as phonetic a spelling as his Welsh ear heard. The word eventually evolved into Maui after 1820 when New England missionaries altered the native language from the somewhat Tahitian dialect, and put the new Hawaiian language into writing.

Captain Cook also did something that surprised the Hawaiians -- he named all the islands as a group calling them The Sandwich Islands. This grouping of islands as if they should be one nation was a European idea, and it flew in the face of the original Polynesian settlers of islands in the Pacific. Hawaiians never named these islands as a group. Each island was individually named and thought of as a separate kingdom. This was true of all islands in the Polynesia, Micronesia and Melanesia Pacific.

Maui's nick-name is 'The Valley Isle." Today people refer to the "valley" as the low land connecting Haleakala with West Maui mountains.

Wrong.

Way back when the name was first proposed, it was to designate the fact that Maui had more valleys (many were really gulches) than any other Hawaiian Island. The low land connecting the two ends of Maui is an isthmus.

* * *

But let's begin our tour of this special island. We will explore Kahului and Wailuku in the northeast first, then south and west Maui; power up to Haleakala Volcano via upcountry Kula, and then mosey around to Hana and Kipahulu in the east. Don't worry, we shall proceed completely around both ends of Maui on those narrow, seldom driven (Ha!) roads that the rental car companies warn you about.

KAHULUI

Kahului is either a suburb of the airport or of the old town of Wailuku. I have not yet decided which. All three today are connected by continuous buildings and traffic lights at intersections, whereas in the past they were separated by country. The airport was beyond the tidal fishponds through a forest of keawe trees. Wailuku was far up the hill through sugarcane fields. Now it is all one city growing sideways with housing developments, light industrial areas, community and state projects, and shopping centers.

The first thing you will probably notice is that Kahului is stained red. Dirt red. (Tourist shops sell a T-shirt stained with this dirt.) The color comes from sugarcane field soil that blows through Kahului after a harvest. Back around the mid-1800s, the area was once all sugar fields from four original plantations. Slowly they are being pushed back to accept development.

First to be developed was Kahului harbor and a railway (1881, the first in the islands) from the sugar mills to the harbor. Then a few houses and a store. Growth here was slow. When the first tour book of Maui was used by visitors in 1875, Kahului was not even mentioned. In 1900 what there was of the settlement was deliberately burned due to the bubonic plague.

The military moved into central Maui in a big way during World War II. They created Pu'unene Naval Air Station, which today is Kahului airport. After Oahu, the military left its largest impact on Maui. Over five war years, more than 200,000 men trained on central Maui. They outnumbered the resident population of the island 4 to 1.

After 1946 Kahului really came into its own. Today's visitor can shop, frequent its restaurants, and on Saturday morning discover the combination swap meet, flea market, farmer's market, whatever, in among the ironwood trees on Pu'unene Road.

I hit this public market one Saturday and struck gold. In a cardboard box filled more or less with junk, I found an old black and white photograph of Kealakekua Bay on the Big Island showing the monument where Captain James Cook was killed. After running the photo through the Hawaii State Archives, I learned it was taken in 1888 when King Kalakaua visited the site. Only one other photo was known to exist of this event, and that one was shot from a different perspective. The photo I bought was taken from the rigging of a sailing ship stationed more or less where Captain Cook had anchored his Discovery and Resolution. The photo showed the monument and the royal party along with several houses nearby that no one remembers ever having been built. Hawaiians were out in the bay in outrigger canoes.

***

There are many, many good swimming beaches on Maui. One in Kahului bordering the airport is a well-kept local secret. This is Kanaha Beach Park, an extremely well-maintained county park with good bath houses. The best part is a waterfront tailor-made for younger children. Although it is on the windward side of Maui, no high surf pounds onto the beach due to a natural barrier reef offshore. The safety aspect of the water draws windsurfing enthusiasts to learn the sport and develop their skills here before braving other more challenging areas.

Baldwin Beach Park just east of Kahului Airport is considered part of the city. As beaches go, it is considered one of the best on Windward Maui. Very used by the local folks.

Maui residents are protective of their beaches and shoreline. Recently, Mauians turned down a proposal for a dolphin facility to share Kanaha Beach. The promoters said the operation would create jobs and be a tourist draw, but the public felt they had too few beaches as it was, and turned them down flat.

I realize that most visitors come to Maui for the beaches, but a few do not. These short-timers only have a few days to experience as much of the island as possible. This means putting up in a hotel and driving, driving, driving to the various parts of the island for sightseeing. For these visitors, I suggest staying in a hotel in Kahului or Kihei. This way they can parcel up the island for their drive to Hana, to Haleakala for the sunrise, and to the south and west shores without a lot of extra backtracking. If they stay far out in Lahaina or Ka'anapali, they are

10

forever having to put on 60 or more extra miles a day before beginning any of the other trips.

***

Inland from the beach, and bordering the airport, is Kanaha Pond Wildlife Sanctuary, one of the more important wetlands in our State. It is one of the most productive areas in Hawaii for two endangered species of birds: the Hawaiian stilt and Hawaiian coot. Wildlife biologists are currently trying to get native vegetation to regain its dominance in this area.

WAILUKU

This is the county seat with government buildings, historic churches, mission houses, and an aging commercial district. One building after another is empty (compared to 1960). New business centers are in Kahului. But like Hilo on The Big Island, Wailuku has charm. Side streets leading off Main Street offer specialty stores of island products priced just right. It's a refreshing trend after you have gone in and out of a dozen stores in the vacation districts looking for that special something that does not shout "bought in a tourist trap." There are things here that do not have "Maui" written all over them.

There's a refreshing commercial trend not only in Wailuku, but especially in resort tourist areas. There are retirees on Maui who are not ready to retire. Many who had owned upscale businesses on the Mainland or in other countries have rented shop space and re-entered the marketplace. They have money, experience, and connections to buy the brands of goods they wish to sell, and at the same time give the customer expert and individual attention. They don't worry about being in competition with anyone.

They plan to live here until they die, and in the meantime aim to keep busy and satisfy their customers. They clearly intend to put commercial Maui on a higher plane than the ever-present honkytonk franchise shops where one size fits all. This speciality service applies to things like clothing, sporting equipment, or household items. It includes bakeries, hobby services, and even photo finishing. You might think that those one-day photo finishing shops are all alike. Well, they aren't. Wait until you find one operated by this new breed of Maui resident! You will return home and keep sending film there to be developed and printed.

I read somewhere that Maui has no parking meters. People boast about this because it gives a feeling of "we are still not heavily commercial as other places." Yes, there are no parking meters on streets, but there are parking meters in Wailuku. I couldn't go to the Public Library without feeding one.

A portion of Wailuku has been designated a State Historic District, the second one in our State. The first was Lahaina. The original churches, missionary homes, and mission station are the focus in Wailuku's historic area. A visit to them is well worth your time, especially the Bailey Museum.

IAO NEEDLE?

Iao Valley stretches behind Wailuku with the road ending at a series of steps that take visitors to a view of Iao Needle, a 1,600 pinnacle of rock. Mark Twain thought this spear of rock should be the monument to Captain Cook because it was the most imposing natural landmark he had seen.

Iao Needle is not a single towering spear of

rock. It is only the first high point on a long winding knife-edge ridge that travels onward up the valley. There are other high points along the ridge, but because of the angle from which the visitor views the ridge from inside the narrow valley, Iao Needle looks as if it is just one pinnacle of rock. An aerial view shows no imposing towering rock at all.

The valley is historic in many respects. It was the major taro growing area of West Maui and therefore of prime importance to Hawaiians. The sacred bones of many Hawaiian royalty were buried in caves around there. When Maui was invaded by kings of other islands, the focal point of attack was usually this general area. More often than not, the invading army was successfully routed by the Maui forces before they got to the valley.

But not King Kamehameha the First from the island of Hawaii in the summer of 1790 when he made his move to capture Maui in his bid for all the Hawaiian islands. He was only successful in conquering Maui (and all the other islands except Kauai) because he was aided by western armament and foreign trainers to use the new weapons. Cannons mounted on carriages did the job at Wailuku.

This battle in Iao Valley has come down to us in legend and chants because historians claim it was the hardest contested battle on Hawaiian record. The best report is by Abraham Fornander, former Circuit Judge of Maui County who married a chiefess from Moloka'i, and put together an impressive history of Hawaii from the Hawaiian point of view in the mid to late 1800s. He got his story from people who witnessed the battle.

The visitor to this narrow valley might pause

14

and reflect on what went on around him 200 years ago.

The battle began just below Wailuku town with Kamehameha's forces coming from the sea. As the battle began, women, children and the aged from all of central Maui were sent onto the mountain sides of Iao Valley where they could watch and hear the fighting below.

Fornander writes: "The eye-witnesses speak of the carnage as frightful, the din and uproar (of the cannon), the shouts of defiance among the fighters, the wailing of the women on the crests of the valley, as something to curdle the blood or madden the brain of the beholder."

Can you just imagine Iao Valley being a modern football stadium where the crowd in the bleachers cheered on their warrors, and then wailed at their deaths as perhaps 5,000 or more men fought on the floor of the valley? The booming of the cannon bouncing off the valley walls was probably just as demoralizing to the Maui army as the killing. It is said that the slaughter was so great that the bodies of the dead dammed the river.

I always figured that statement was a little much, so I once walked the river to try and visualize that happening. Yes, it could happen. In one spot, I came across a narrow place where ripe guavas had fallen from trees. The yellow fruit floating on the water lodged against rocks making a virtual dam.

***

Below the Needle are two possible items worth investigating.

The first is a nature center complex, that at the time this book was written, seemed to be part museum, part amusement park, part educational center, all having something to do with things of nature. I liked what I saw, and it was interesting.

Below was a County Park called Heritage Gardens that looks inviting for strolling. The grounds are divided into five plots, each given to an ethnic theme with traditional plantings and a building. Represented are the Filipino, Japanese, Portuguese, Caucasians, and Hawaiians. (For some reason the Chinese are missing. I wonder about this because Maui as a whole is lacking in things Chinese. Even the number of Chinese restaurants are few on Maui compared to the other islands.)

Anyway, in walking this non-beach park and other botanical parks (State and County) around Maui, I come to an unfortunate conclusion. These parks seemed to have been planned and initially executed with a grand idea, but somewhere along the line, interest (or lack of money) died. The parks sit there seemingly unfinished or underdeveloped. Workers come and clean the grounds, but that's all. I for one, expected more in the way of enlightment and education at Heritage Gardens because this park has a theme, and I come away unfulfilled. It's time for a wakeup call to Maui County. We are entering the age of eco-tourism, and much more will be expected from our parks.

SOUTH MAUI

Generally known as Kihei, the coastal area consists of six sub-districts spread over 20 miles of coastline: Kealia, Kihei, Kama'ole, Wailea, Makena, and La Perouse. There are 18 good swimming beaches along this coast.

While this area has a history, what the visitor sees today stems from about 1950. Before that, south Maui was an overly warm area of dusty brown grass and keawe trees. Here and there were miniature oases of greenery surrounding long-established churches and a few beach houses.

Land here after World War II sold for $250 an acre. Today a one bedroom condo costs well over $150,000. The monthly maintenance fee per apartment is $250 to keep plants watered, grass mowed, swimming pool vacuumed, and the building painted once every 20 years.

You approach this area either from Kahului, Wailuku, or Lahaina through wide-open land, sugar fields, and scrub trees. This is fast going to change. Possibly by the time this book gets into another printing there will be two thousand homes, a golf course, schools, and a shopping center at the entrance of Kihei.

***

At the western end of this shore is Kealia wildlife sanctuary, a somewhat swampy, salt marsh. What water ponds here either comes from rain or from under the ground. Ocean water floods upward with the tide. When these floods happen, several species of birds (like the leggy Hawaiian Stilt) can be viewed and photographed if you are lucky enough to get close. Otherwise, the area will appear lifeless and smell of pickles from the *akulikuli* ground cover.

Only recently is the area being developed too attract wildlife, and the visitor to view it. Elevated boardwalks and interpretive exhibits are planned.

TURTLES CROSSING

One event here gets Maui residents in an uproar. That's when the endangered hawksbill turtle comes onto Maalaea beach to lay its eggs. Sometimes turtles cross the highway to bury their eggs in marsh sand. Speeding cars handled by sightless drivers run over the turtles, and this makes headlines in the island's newspaper. All hell becomes unhinged when the baby turtles hatch and head for the ocean by crossing the road, always at night. During that time, squads of citizens patrol the area all night to direct traffic.

During World War II, Marines used this beach and swamp land to practice amphibian assaults for such target areas as Saipan, the Marianas and Iwo Jima. These practice sessions continued up to about 1960. Maui and the military did not recognize this area as a possible wildlife refuge. It was useless land. Useless, except for military exercises. Even as recently as 1959, flotillas of Navy ships would line the horizon and let loose a mess of landing craft full of Marines and their equipment. The forces would hit this beach, and tanks, trucks, jeeps, you name it, would scurry inland to capture Maui.

KIHEI

Kihei has two main roads along its length. One borders the ocean, the other inland where other housing, commercial, and golf course development has started, and will someday span the countryside. Today, the beach road has more or less wall-to-wall condos interspaced with commercial centers. What private homes exist here today will be replaced tomorrow with highrises.

First hotel built along here was a Canadian enterprise, the Maui Lu. Today, owned by other interests, it is showing its age gracefully. In the early 1960s, my wife helped design and build the hotel's cottages. We always had a warm feeling for the hotel, and today that feeling continues with the new managers, the Howard Johnson group. You see, my wife's father went to school with the original Howard Johnson of Boston.

***

Continuing down Kihei's waterfront, we come to Kama'ole Beach I, II and III, beach parks that rightly are the gems of Maui County. A visitor must go far and wide on any Hawaiian island to find better swimming beaches. In fact, these beaches are an example (along with others in Wailea and Ka'anapali) of why Maui is so popular with visitors, despite the fact that of all major Hawaiian islands, it is the most expensive to visit.

In a recent two year period I made a survey of about 2,000 vacationers around our State (some 300 in a 30-day period on Maui in September 1996), to discover what makes this island so special. The reason is simple. It is the combination of a condo or resort room, a good beach with safe swimming, and the selection of excellent restaurants and shopping - all within easy reach - and of course dry, warm weather. The key is that these are all in close proximity to each other. In other words, "I can see all these assets from my room balcony, and walk to each."

There is one more item. The view from every room is of at least two or three other Hawaiian islands just across the ocean. This gives the visitor the feeling of being on an island in the islands. It is psychologically important as it confirms the fact that they are truely on a Pacific island. (For residents, the closeness of these islands gives protection from hurricane winds and tidal waves.)

The average comment we heard from visitors in 1996 was: "Of course there is sightseeing atop Haleakala and on the way to Hana. These are all-day adventures. Once you have done them, the traveling is over. You zero in on what you came to Hawaii for - relaxation at the beach, a good comfortable room, good food, and other island scenery any time you glance toward the ocean."

That's the time-honored image of a Hawaiian vacation. It works for the first time visitor, and certainly is a secret of having them return year after year.

***

All the popular beaches have lifeguards. I watched, and watched, and watched for weeks and

20

never saw a lifeguard leave his tower. Finally, I went up to one guard and asked, "If a person ever got into trouble on this beach, what would it be? Shark attack? Cramps? Heart attack?"

"None of the above," the guard answered. "Water conditions on leeward Maui are too ideal. When something happens, it is usually a child or older person caught off guard by a wave and knocked down. In their surprise, they momentarily panic in the surf."

WAILEA

Next to Kama'ole is Wailea, a district of exciting upscale resorts bounded on one side by miles of golf course, and on the other by handy beaches and good swimming. Wailea hotels and what they offer continually rate number one in the world for the discriminating vacationer. The grounds here are landscaped and pruned to death by an army of workers. I get the feeling that no flower or leaf is allowed to fall from a bush or tree, and if it does, it cannot remain on the ground for more than 12 hours. The grass cannot grow more than an eighth of an inch. If the wind blows, it's probably filtered. God help a bird that does his job on a sidewalk.

I think: Does all this groundskeeping make things look extra pretty? Or does it look more artificial?

Speaking of plantings around condos and resorts:

Yard crews hired to keep the place manicured are really mowers and choppers. Horticultural practices are foreign to them. Types of trees and bushes are planted where they should not be. When the botanical item grows into its god-given glory, the

21

condo owners find that it:

1. Blocks their view of the ocean or Haleakala Volcano.

2. Buffers the breeze from wafting though their condo to keep them reasonably cool.

3. Makes a mess on concrete walks and on cars in the parking lot.

Therefore, the yard crew's job is to so severely chop out the botanical goodness that the tree becomes unrecognizable as to its species and what spectacular items it is supposed to produce. Shrubbery that would flower remains a green wall.

One tree that every hotelier who has been in Hawaii long enough to unpack his bags knows should not be planted within a mile of his hotel --- the Chinese banyan. First of all, if you view the banyan in Lahaina's downtown waterfront, you will note that it can grow to cover half a city block. Secondly, it is the all-time favorite sports stadium and karioke stage of the mynah bird. The raucous squawking of millions of those birds can occur in a banyan from dawn to 9 a.m. and from 4 p.m. to well after dark.

In the specific case of the Wailea district, potentially beautiful monkeypod trees were planted on both sides of the highway for mile after mile. But you would not recognize the tree if you walked right into it. Beyond being prized for making furniture, bowls, and trays, the tree's magnificence comes from its massive umbrella shape. The Wailea monkeypods are pruned to grow more like a coconut tree. No side branching limbs. The tree looks like something out of Africa that's been eaten almost to its top branches by giant giraffes.

I was told that yard service people have contracts for so many hours each week per condo, when every other week would be adequate. Quite often condo owners see landscape maintenance guys "chopping the air with their clippers" to put in their time.

And while we are on this subject, the official flower of Maui is a pink damask rose from Asia Minor that arrived here in the early 1800s. It was given the name Maui Rose, or Lokelani, and was once grown widely in upcountry Kula and Ulupalakua. Today the rose is rarely seen. It has been replaced by a poor substitute variety of a common pink rose.

So why is this rose still the official flower of Maui, when there is another flower grown in almost every yard, on every golf course, and in front of every condo window on Maui? It is the Singapore plumeria, white with a yellow center. This should be the official flower of the island.

Here's a little-known fact. You know, of course, that each Hawaiian Island has an official flower. They were chosen in 1923 when the Territorial Legislature passed a joint resolution designating official emblems for the each of the islands. So, what is the flower of tiny Molokini island, that popular snorkling island off Wailea? Molokini has only a succulent called *Molokini Ihi* in the way of vegetation. It's emblem is sea foam.

END OF THE ROAD

After Wailea comes Makena and Maui's longest, widest, pure white sand beach. They simply call it "The Big Beach." Good for sunbathing, swimming and body surfing, but with caution as sometimes there's an undertow. Over a headland of lava is Little Beach which in the past was a clothing optional one. It offers good surfing.

These beaches gained notoriety about 40 years ago when the hippie culture discovered the area was the culmination of their South Seas dream, and attempted to live in the keawe bush bordering the beaches. It was scenic utopia. Local residents also liked to spend the summer tenting here. Since then, Maui officials have had a battle keeping the place public without squatters. Today, there are parking lots at both ends of the beach. A caretaker's residence is planned which will give the County better control.

***

The shoreline beyond Big Beach to La Perouse Bay features one rocky cove after another. This is do-it-yourself snorkeling country where fish and coral abound. The waters are mainly waveless. The area is unsupervised, so don't snorkel alone.

Homes of the wealthy hug the shoreline wherever possible. Their gates display signs on which *KAPU* is written in large letters. The need to hide from the passing public seems to be the deal, and every owner builds a high lava rock wall to shield his property.

One day I watched as local workers built one of these walls. They were building it of a'a lava, using pieces of basalt half the size of a tennis ball that obviously came from the nearby lava flow at La Perouse.

"Do you know what's gonna happen to that wall in 40 years?" I asked one worker.

"Yep. It's gonna turn into dirt."

"So why build it?"

"The rich haole man thinks it looks good. The rock is cheap and easy to get. And anyway, he'll be dead long before the 40 years."

***

Having driven this far, many visitors anticipate something grand at the end of the road at La Perouse. There is a modest monument to the famous French explorer Captain J.F.G. de La Perouse who visited here for a day eleven years after Captain Cook. The road ends in a parking area. A jeep road does continue, but degenerates now and then into a trail. Walking here is okay, and exploring the shoreline and its tidal pools is rewarding. But know one thing. An unattended parked car is an invitation to vandals in many rural places on Maui.

Warnings concerning thefts from tourist vehicles and rooming facilities are posted in most sightseeing publications, and it is a concern that some visitors apparently don't take seriously. Crime against tourists rises in direct relationship to the number of residents and visitors. (Maui is the fastest growing island in our state in both respects.) Today crime has also appeared on Lanai in a meaningful way since that island went from agriculture to tourism.

This theft problem became so great in south Maui that the county started a Citizens Patrol program in 1995, and today the program is being greatly expanded. Lately, five new police officers were hired specifically to combat crimes against visitors. In 1996, a joke (that really wasn't a joke) made its way through the community. Kihei firemen responded to a brush fire in Wailea and were absent from their station for most of the day. While they were away, someone burgled their lockers in the station. "Now we have to babysit the fire station when there's a fire," was the joke.

My suggestion from owning a visitor industry company for 23 years, and running a Bed and Breakfast home for the last 14 years: When arriving on any island, make every effort to check into your accommodation and leave your bags there before going sightseeing. Take only the few necessities while touring, things like your camera and money. And when leaving the car for a walk, take everything with you. Belted butt bags are an excellent idea instead of carrying a purse or shoulder bag which you might have to put down somewhere and step away from it.

MOLOKINI ISLE

The small boat harbor at Ma'alaea is a busy place in the mornings, and will be much busier in the future as there are plans to greatly expand the harbor. A 20-million gallon aquarium called the Maui Ocean Center is being built on 18 acres, along with a village shopping center. It will be the sixth Coral World International Aquarium patterned after those in the U.S. Virgin Islands, the Bahamas, Austrialia and the Red Sea. It will offer a Whale Discovery Center and a Marine Science Center.

Many boats leave various boat harbors such as Ma'alaea for Molokini island with snorkeling and whale watching parties. Other sport fishing boats put to sea. Most of them will be back by lunch time because of the trade wind pattern over the waters off south Maui. The ocean is mirror calm in the mornings, but by noon the wind rises and boating becomes uncomfortable.

**

There are nine marine preserves in Hawaii, but Molokini lying 2.7 miles off Maui, is the only "offshore" preserve. The island is a "tuft cone" that was once like Diamond Head at Waikiki, only most of it collapsed into the ocean, leaving a horseshoe rim.

27

(Molokini has a clone in Kaela island off Niihau). I
am telling you these facts because I have a story
about Molokini. This tiny island has a special
memory for me. Fifty years ago I was involved in
blowing the island up. Honest.

It all began with the battle of Midway in 1942.
Up to then, Army and Navy Air Force pilots bombed
enemy ships by diving straight at them hoping that
the dropped bomb would land smack on the ship.
Better yet, down the smoke stack. This seldom
happened as the American plane was usually so close
to the ship that it was shot down.

So a new bomb and technique of dive bombing
were perfected. The idea came from what kids do who
stand on the shore of a calm lake, and finding small
flat stones at the water's edge, sidehand the stone so
that it skips along the surface of the water. The new
torpedo-like bomb was slung under the belly of the
dive bomber, and when the plane pulled out of its dive
some distance off to the side of an enemy ship, the
bomb would pancake on the ocean and skip into the
side of the ship. The plane and crew could then pull
away from the action at a safe distance and escape.

Where to find a "ship" to practice on? Why,
Molokini Island of course. The island was a natural
because the Naval Air Station was on Maui. And so
that tiny narrow crescent of a barren island was
bombed and blasted for years.

But then, as World War II ended, the Territory
of Hawaii wanted targets on Kauai, Oahu, and Maui,
(other than Kaho'olawe,) cleared of dud ammunition
so the public could again use these special areas. I
was in the Army Engineers 25th Division demolition
squad that did such things.

Our squad was taken to Molokini on a Navy

light buoy tender. But because the ship had a hectic schedule of repairs around the Pacific, we were allowed only one day to clear the island of all unexploded ordinance. How to do this?

The way we figured was to find all the duds, remove the impact firing mechanisms in the nose, fill the cavity with fresh dynamite, insert a fuse, and then link the bombs together with an explosive cord. In that way, we could light one fuse and blow all the bombs at one time. About 10 hours of daylight was all the time we had to do the job.

The Navy landed us on Molokini from an open lifeboat launch. The crew of that launch then went off fishing. The light tender we had come over on from Pearl Harbor was anchored about a mile away.

By 3 p.m. we had linked all the bombs. There were hundreds of them. To blow them up, we figured we had to either get off the island via the launch, or find a place to hide on the island. We chose to stay on the island since we had discovered a shallow cave at the water's edge.

So we lit a 20-minute fuse and all 12 of us went for cover in the cave. The countdown had six minutes to go when we heard the putt-putt-putt of a motor. Around the corner of Molokini came the launch with four crewmen trolling fishing lines, singing and carrying on in grand style as sailors do during rest and recreation time.

I ran out of the cave and yelled, "Get the hell out of here. Go. Go. Get as far away from here as you can."

They waved back, laughed, and continued their merry way around the corner of the island.

Molokini blew up with a tremendous roar. A dense gray/green cloud erupted, darkened the sky and blew off leeward. Rocks of every imaginable size went flying. No explosion so far in World War II impressed me as much as the eruption of Molokini. It took the atomic bomb to make a better impression later.

The explosion cloud drifted over the launch, and for the next few minutes all we heard was the putt, putt, putting of the motor. When the cloud lifted, no one could be seen in the boat. Rocks rained down all over the ocean.

"Oh, my God," I shouted. "They're all dead."

When the rocks stopped falling, one by one heads appeared over the rail. They were all okay.

I think the falling rocks impressed me the most. I never knew rocks could fly so far. A mile away the Navy tender received direct hits. We heard harsh words from her skipper later. In fact, he was all for sailing away and leaving us on the island.

But the heaviest complaint came from the Mayor of Maui. Rocks thudded on roofs, rained down on beaches all over La Perouse, Makena, and Wailea. The Mayor made a big stink about it, and I believe this is where the idea was first born in Maui County that the military should stop bombing the Island of Kaho'olawe and return it to Territorial control.

About 20 years ago it was discovered that the area around Molokini was great for snorkeling. Today some 10 companies working out of Lahaina, Ma'alaea and Kihei offer snorkeling trips to the island. I shuddered at this. We had cleared the island of dud ordinance, but had not checked the waters around Molokini. In 1975 the Navy exploded two bombs found in the water, and in 1988 two more bombs were dragged far out into deep water.

WEST MAUI

The first leg of the highway to Lahaina and Ka'anapali curves around cliffs and through a tunnel. There are two interesting sights along this route.

At the beginning you will notice an unpaved road leading to a small, low marine light. If you are from Scandinavia, you will drive onto this road and discover the only monument to your countrymen in Hawaii. Six hundred Norwegians, Swedes and Danes arrived off this spot on Feb. 18, 1881, in the Norwegian Barque *Beta*. They were destined to work the sugar plantations. It was the only such migration of its kind in Hawaii's history.

All along this cliffy route uphill from the modern highway are abandoned sections of the former highway. The old construction is fascinating. An example of one section is pictured by Joann in an oil painting in the center of this book.

Next, the highway now flattens out and runs beside the ocean all the way to Lahaina. Most of the waterfront is undeveloped public park. You are welcome to stop anywhere to picnic, swim, or walk the waterfront to your heart's content.

The only break along this lovely shore view is the former settlement of Olowalu where there is a country store. In the hills at the back used to be

31

Maui's best representation of pictographs, or
Hawaiian rock art. No more. The art has been so
damaged that the landowner, Pioneer Mill, has put
the area off limits.

DISASTER

The name Olowalu is etched in history
because the biggest massacre of Hawaiians by an
early foreign ship happened here in February 1790.
About 100 Hawaiians from Lahaina, Ka'anapali,
Lanai, and villages along this shore were killed
outright, and another 100 or so injured, many of
whom died later. A Hawaiian chief from Olowalu
stole a cutter tied to the American ship Eleanor
during the night (in a copycat action of what
happened to Captain Cook in 1779 on the island of
Hawaii.) In retaliation, the captain lured the natives
to trade along one side of the ship, then blew
everyone out of the water with his deck cannons.
    An untold story goes with this killing.
    This tragic event at Olowalu was written down
and circulated among ships' captains for years
afterward. Twenty-two years later the deed was
remembered and reenacted against Indians off the
west coast of Vancouver Island, British Columbia.
More than 300 Indians were killed, and an entire
generation of native men was erased from this section
of Vancouver Island.
    The Northwest incident had a more
imaginative twist than the Maui killing. Indians
tried to overpower the crew of the ship, but were
driven off after many seamen were killed. The
captain and the rest of the crew escaped in a smaller

boat in the middle of the night leaving a seriously injured man hiding below decks. This sailor rigged the ship into a time bomb using barrels of powder. When the Indians returned with reinforcements the next day, they swarmed aboard ship, and the entire ship was blown sky high. Not a single Indian survived.

What makes this incident even more interesting is that this ship had 12 Hawaiians aboard as seamen. None survived the Indian attack.

LAHAINA

Lahaina is many things to many people. Take your pick:

* Historic - the first capitol of the Hawaiian Kingdom, home of royalty, one scene of the whaling industry, and an important missionary outpost.

* Artistic - Where many towns have more real estate offices per square block, Lahaina has more art galleries.

* Honky tonk with palm trees - wall to wall tourist items, many mass-produced in the Orient. (But be on the lookout for those kamaaina shops I mentioned earlier.)

* Water sportsville - offering everything from sails to Lana'i, to sport fishing, parasailing, snorkeling, whale watching, surfing, kayaking, water skiing, etc.

Of the above, the historical aspect of Lahaina is one that lures the visitor.

The County of Maui commissioned a detailed historical study in 1961 to get Lahaina set aside as Hawaii's first historical district. They had a plan for what features should be restored, and how much it might cost. The restoration would recreate the look of Lahaina during the hundred and eighty years between 1736 and 1915.

Thirty-one restoration features were proposed. Only 12 have been acted upon over the years.

The original plan, along with estimated cost, had a slogan: "If Maui wants it, it can be done."

Apparently, official Maui never wanted it bad enough. They had a grand idea, but no will or assignment of a budget to make it happen.

In preparation for this book, I took the Lahaina Historical Restoration and Preservation Plan in one hand, the current visitor guide to historic Lahaina in the other, and made the tour. Joann and I became frustrated knowing what the restoration adventure could be today.

The truly sad part is that only one of the historic Hawaiian monarchy features (a portion of the old fort's wall) has been recreated. The missionary and some whaling aspects of Lahaina were addressed. Other ethnic groups are now represented through their churches in the area. Modern needs, such as a public library, school, a ball field and playground, hotel, and shopping center all built on former native settlements, have since made sure that the Hawaiian historical aspect of Lahaina will never be restored in place. However, in the future, some of Lahaina's royal heritage may be reproduced elsewhere in the area now that the Hawaiian cultural movement is strong.

Roy Nickerson's book "*Lahaina, Royal Capital of Hawaii*," is great for those wishing to understand the history of this town. In his last chapter, "Lahaina Today," he faced the same problem I am in writing about its historic restoration. He concluded, "More than the exact duplication of the past, however, (it) {the Maui County Historic Commission} acts to preserve that which remains of the old, and then works toward preserving the atmosphere within which modern Lahaina can build .... and with mixed results."

Translation: Not one thing remains of the era from 1736 to 1820. Only one item was symbolically restored, in part - the Fort on the Canal. Several missionary homes and structures remained from the period 1820 to 1870, so these too were restored, and ethnic churches that date from after 1900 are now included in the historical lineup. And so Lahaina appears today with a historical atmosphere of mixed results.

What has been restored, or kept in good repair by local historical committies working with private grants and their own hard earned money, is excellent and worth visiting. These include the missionary homes, the Courthouse, banyan tree square, the Old Prison, the lighthouse, Hale Aloha and Hale Pa'ahao. Items added, like the sailing ship Carthaginian on the waterfront go a long way to give the district its historical atmosphere.

Otherwise, the visitor takes a self-guided tour via signs that sometimes forces them try to visualize something they know nothing about. I would do away with at least three of these signs, and re-do the commercial visitor's guide. King Kamehameha's taro patch, which wasn't there in the first place, (the representation of a dry concrete foot bath is an embarrassment); The Hauola Stone which wasn't there either, (stones at the bottom of a sea wall are confusing); and the scholar and first Hawaiian historian David Malo's Home, which was never of historic value, and not where they say it is today.

***

As for the rest of Lahaina, you might walk the shops on Front Street, have an ice cream, and be charmed by the offerings in the numerous art galleries. There are some excellent artists on Maui.

Now a word on the Pioneer Inn. The present owner says that it is "the oldest hotel in Hawaii," (1902) and that, "His ancestor built it ALL from scratch in the spot it is in today."

This may, or may not be the entire story, but until someone presents clearer facts through research, I buy the following:

The Maunalei Sugar Company began business on the coast of Lana'i facing Lahaina in 1899. They built a spacious two story building with a wraparound veranda that looked something like the Pioneer Inn does today. Within it was the plantation office, a company store, rooms for visitors, and a company boarding facility. Wells that produced brackish water, and an outbreak of bubonic plague doomed the plantation in two short years. The building was left standing until 1905, then dismantled a section at a time and floated on rafts to Lahaina. There it was hammered together again, changed somewhat, and ADDED to the Pioneer Inn which was started in 1902.

KA'ANAPALI

Onward to Ka'anapali and beyond. The visitor destination district you are about to motor through is parceled into five sections: Ka'anapali, Honokowai, Kahana, Napili and Kapalua. All contain golf courses, resorts, and condos, with some residential housing.

This was once heavy sugar and pineapple country. As every resident on Maui knows, sugar people torch the fields on calm nights, or early in the morning, to rid the plants of dry leaves and to heat the stock which starts the sugar flowing as the first step toward processing. Black ash floats on high and eventually settles over homes and squeezes through window screens to coat furniture. My fondest memory as a child on neighboring Moloka'i was to be awakened sometime after midnight by my mother to go sit on the front porch and watch the "volcano eruption" on west Maui. The fields would flare up, and from afar resemble a lava flow coming down a volcanic slope.

The beaches and water are calm on the Ka'napali coast on the leeward, southwestern edge of west Maui, but toward the end of this drive we begin to enter the windward coast where fresh trade winds stir things up. Lana'i and Moloka'i are the scenic islands offshore.

Most of this shoreline was developed beginning in the late 1950s by the landowner American Factors. Their first effort at Ka'anapali started modern tourism on Maui. What they did also set the trend for visitor accommodations statewide.

Since many of these resorts are now older, the landscaping has mellowed compared to Wailea, and plantings look more like they should.

This section of the island has an airport for non-jet planes. As tourism grows with new resorts like Kapalua, pressure within the industry is to enlarge the airport to accept jets. Residents stand up and say, "No way!" (Oh, it will come. Not this year, or the next, but it will happen.)

AROUND NORTH MAUI

The road you are on continues around the northern end of west Maui and then back to Kahului. Beyond Kapalua there are two deep, sheltered bays that draw snorkelers: Honolua and Honokohau. (Here again are car theft problems.)

Beyond, the road curves through cattle grazing country, up, down and around, through gulches, alongside cliffs, through Kahakuloa valley, over more mountainous rugged terrain, and finally dips down into urban central Maui.

The partially paved road is only 23 miles long, but it will take you hours and hours as the average speed limit should be 15 miles an hour. The road is wide enough for only one car in many places, so remember, cars going uphill have the right of way. Blow your horn at blind corners. Wave a thank you, and smile, smile, smile. This road is an adventure, not a test.

It's fun to play a character game along this road. Make eye contact with the driver and passengers as you slowly creep past a car going in the opposite direction. Some drivers will have concern parked on their faces, and you just know they are saying, "Why am I taking this drive?" Others are bored because they live in the mountains of Colorado and this type of road is common. Some drivers will be smiling, but with a sick smile that says they hope to get though this without dinging up the rental car. Passengers will glance your way, and you know from their rigid posture that they would rather get out and walk.

Relax. It's an interesting drive.

Twenty years ago I drove this road (unpaved then) and didn't meet one car coming or going. Back then, rental car companies put the fear of the Lord into their clients. Dire things were sure to happen if you attempted this drive. This year I kept count, and during the three hours it took me to amble along, (stopping in a scenic place to have a picnic) I counted 88 rental cars on this road. And it was a weekday!

***

Midway on this route is a surprise --- the remote village of Kahakuloa. No place could be more picturesque. A collection of houses, some built in the 1920s, others more modern but allowed to weather and blend into the landscape. Newly painted old church. Original rock walls built over a century ago still guarding each house plot. Taro patches still in use. The old school is gone and replaced by a community center of sorts.

Quiet hovers over the scene. The settlement fills the lower part of a valley where a good-size stream flows year long. This stream once made the village one of the more populated on Maui due to its food production. And being isolated, it never figured in the problems and wars around the rest of Maui. Since the mid-1800s it has enjoyed the status of a romantic get-away that allows feelings to return to yesteryear. Kahakuloa was self-suffcent with church, school, taro and rice patches, a canoe launching beach for fishing, wild fruit, and a field or two for horses and cattle. Eras of progress have come and gone with Kahakuloa changing with the times, but somehow it hasn't changed that much -- if you don't want it to change. Kahakuloa is forever Kahakuloa.

KULA

The word Kula means plain, field, open country or pasture, and that's exactly what the Kula district is on the slope of Haleakala Volcano. But it has another connotation. The word also is associated with "coolness," as in comfortable living without air conditioning, where anything you plant in your yard grows to perfection, and there's a scenic view over central and west Maui that will not stop. This image of a perfect island district comes instantly to mind wherever in Hawaii (or for that matter, anywhere in the world) you might mention Kula. For people working all their lives in a place like Honolulu, the name conjures up dreams of retirement.

Locally, the entire higher altitude of the west and south slopes of Haleakala is know as "Up Country." And as it is with special places, it eventually becomes identified in a time frame by an individual who embodies the spirit and love of the district. In the case of Up Country with its extensive ranching activity, that person is Armine von Tempsky. She was the daughter of Louis von Tempsky of New Zealand who was the manager of Haleakala Ranch back at the turn of this century. Her book, *Born In Paradise,* 1940, has put a stamp forever on the image of upper Haleakala, perhaps on all of Maui.

Many of Armine von Tempsky's books are being newly released today and are available in book stores in paperback. My parents knew the author, and she borrowed my father by name as a character in the book about Hana called *Hula.*

There are four roads to Kula. Two lead through pineapple fields to Makawao, a town that echoes of horses and cowboys. Above the town is the district of Olinda with its towering eucalyptus trees of smooth trunks streaked in pastel shades of green, yellow, and orange. Another road is Maui's newest and eventually takes you to the summit of Haleakala. Still another comes off the isthmus through farms and small ranches.

From Makawao on upward to the 4,000 foot altitude is Kula. You will read how both Irish potatoes and sweet potatoes were grown here as a cash crop for the whaling industry and gold rush days in California. This era was followed by onions and table vegetables. The Kula onion is probably best known as the sweet onion of the Pacific that is eaten like an apple. It is expensive. You'll find them in the market as Maui onions with each marked with a black crayon X. Frank Sinatra orders them by Express Mail.

It is common for visitors to Kula to come away saying "Where were all the farms? I didn't see a single one."

That's true. There are no extensive vegetable farms bordering the major highways through Kula. You have to wander side roads to discover them. When visitors from Nebraska, California, or Florida happen upon one, they breeze right past without blinking, because Hawaii's farms are about the size of backyard vegetable gardens in other states.

More noticeable to the visitor are the flower farms. Kula is the carnation capital of Hawaii. About 1970, along came the protea, a showy blossom from South Africa and Ethiopia that has a long cut flower life, and when dead is suitable for dried arrangements. One species is called the King protea. It comes in pink, or white, or a more common reddish hue, and when fully open can be almost a foot across. One protea flower in a Japanese flower arranger's hands becomes a bouquet. I had a friend who grew King proteas in Kula, and he did okay, but wasn't getting rich. Not that is, until he went to Japan to see what they did with that flower. Growers on Maui were cutting the flower with a short stem thinking they were saving on postage because the flower and stem were heavy. What the Japanese wanted was the stem. So my friend cut his flowers with stems up to two-feet long. He then found he could get $50 a flower!

I hate get rich stories like this if it didn't happen to me. Let's continue to the summit of Haleakala.

HALEAKALA

The road you drive to ascend Maui's ACTIVE volcano was built in 1935. Prior to that, the trip was made by foot or on horseback. Today you might find as many bicycles as autos on the windy road all coming one way -- down. The experience of biking without having to peddle has boomed in the past 10 years, until today no less than eight companies offer their services. I won't tell you the details about the time one biker came whizzing around a corner and splattered onto the front of a delivery truck.

All visitors are bound for the 10,000 foot summit, some in the dark to view the sunrise over the eastern edge of the crater, others later in the morning intent on hiking in the rarified atmosphere. The road is a good two-lane highway with no need for guard rails as pastureland borders it for miles in any direction. While the road is not overly steep, it climbs at a good rate, and you will get to know just how well your rental car company has maintained their engines and transmissions. On many days, usually after noon, the drive will enter a cloud bank at about the 4,000-foot-level, and exit at about 8,000 feet. Please warn passengers that car-sickness is possible due to the curves.

Some fascinating creatures on this volcano

include carnivorous caterpillars, flightless moths, fish that climb 200-foot high waterfalls, giant "picture wing" flies, the largest dragonfly on earth, and a host of colorful birds. These take time and patience to discover. Park rangers hope you do NOT see goats, wild pigs, the mongoose, or wild cats. These introduced species played havoc with endangered wildlife and plants in the past, but today the major portion of the volcano's general summit area has been ringed by a 32-mile fence to keep them out.

HAWAII'S GOOSE

What you might thrill to are two treasures that so far have successfully been brought back from near extinction -- Hawaii's native goose and state bird, the Nene, and a rare exotic plant the Haleakala silversword.

I don't recall where I read it, but someone wrote in a popular scientific work sold on Maui that Nene do not drink water. Another writer claimed the goose does not fly. Perhaps those writers spent time atop Haleakala and saw no ponds or streams, or geese flying, so came to those surprising conclusions. My eyebrows really shot up at this because Nene at Hawaii Volcanoes National Park, where I live, drink water, swim in reservoirs on ranches on Mauna Loa Volcano, and flocks of up to ll geese daily fly in V-formation, honking as they go.

Come to think of it, perhaps geese don't fly all that frequently atop Haleakala. After all, it's 10,000 feet high up there and the atmosphere is thin. They cruise at that altitude when migrating long distances, but it takes them awhile to get up there.

So I went to Haleakala to see Maui's Nene for myself. The first thing I saw were two Nene drinking water from a crack in the highway where a National Park water pipe had a leak and water was running down the crack. A few minutes later in another parking lot I saw a Nene drinking water that had boiled out of an overheated car and pooled on the pavement. Nene drink water on Haleakala, and they find it in the darndest places.

Hawaiians kept these geese as noisy "watch dogs" in their agricultual plots. When Captain James Cook first cruised around the Big Island, he spied several Nene in a canoe when a Hawaiian came to trade shipside. "Get that goose," he ordered. "Tomorrow is Christmas Day and I can have my traditional goose." The goose today is found only at the higher altitudes thanks to the mongoose, other introduced birds, and man, all who provide a lousy atmosphere and habitat for it at lower altitudes.

They say Hawaii's Nene lost some of the web on its feet because the goose, once established here, had no ponds or lakes to swim in, so was doomed to walk around. Well, maybe, but that's not the whole story. One of the Nene's relatives, the Aleutian Goose, has almost the same characteristics as the Nene. It also has the shrunken foot web, the somewhat smaller body size, and the coloring of the Hawaii Goose, because it too does not enjoy ponds or lakes on those volcanic islands.

Oh, by the way, it is not the Hawaiian Goose, but the Hawaii Goose. You don't call the Canada Goose the Canadian Goose, do you?)

GO HIKING

Hiking into, through and around Haleakala is a challenging and popular pastime. Anyone walking into or through this high altitude wonderland should plan the trip ahead of time. It should not be a spur-of- the- moment afterthought. The rewards are great when the adventure is pursued with care and planning.

For instance: there are three overnight cabins on Haleakala's floor, but they are so popular they have to be reserved up to six months or a year in advance. Warm clothes are a must any time of the year. The list of survival items for the length of stay can be endless, and has to be considered while you are in civilization at the lower altitudes. Even hiking down and out of the volcano for a day needs planning.

Of all my excursions into Haleakala, one lingers today as the absolute best. It happened in 1975 when 10 of us were walking around Maui.

We entered Haleakala on the Halemau'u trail which is just above the park's headquarters. (The trail gets its name from the Amau'u fern at the beginning of the trail, whose new leaves are bright red/orange, then turn green when mature.) After spending the day walking across and around cinder cones, we ended up at Kapalaoa cabin centrally located on the crater floor.

Dinner was corned beef, onions, cabbage, and canned peaches at 5 p.m., and by 6 we were asleep.

It was the night of the full moon. We awoke at 2 a.m. and started the walk out by going across the volcano's floor and up Sliding Sands Trail to the summit. Everything was four-dimensonal in the moonlight. The landscape was lit up like an operatic stage. Every rock a prop. Silverswords were brilliant jewels in the distance, or burning bushes of liquid silver up close. Chill air spurred us into a brisk walk. A drifting moon gave life to the towering volcanic walls. Someone remarked, "It's like walking through the pearly gates to your final reward."

The moonlight finally faded as the sun reached out for Hawaii. By this time we were starting up the Sliding Sands Trail. Half way up we walked facing backwards more than forward, concentrating on what was across the crater as the sky brightened to the east. Long pauses to just sit and watch the day arrive were now the thing to do.

Finally the long-awaited moment came, both for us and for half a hundred people waiting in the cold of the summit observation hut on Haleakala's rim. The sun rose over a cloudless eastern rim, a small red ball at first, then a bursting yellow and white spotlight that turned black cinder to an ash brown, gray cones to yellow and red, and towering cliffs to silver and green. I was convinced my angel of mercy had finally arrived.

Twenty minutes later, we were at the summit feeling vastly superior to the tourists who had motored there to see the finale. As far as we were concerned, they had missed the total performance.

EARLY HUMANS ON MAUI

What else can I tell you about Haleakala that you might not get from reading popular literature?

Well, the oldest date for humans on Maui was recorded inside this depression. That surprised archeologists because they were used to finding the oldest habitation under sand dunes at shoreside. To understand this, let me fill you in on Maui's human past.

Human existence has been recorded by evidence uncovered in sand dunes and in lava tube caves found on the Hawaiian Islands. So far the earliest date is shortly after 100 A.D., but archeologists are careful to put into print only what they can absolutely prove, and then are super cautious to err on the conservative side. Therefore, dates like 300, 550, 650 and 750 A.D. keep showing up. Give or take another 20 years as carbon dating gets better, and hopefully as archeologists make new finds, they will pin down a more precise date for the first polynesian arrival. It is whispered behind closed doors that the date could be earlier than now known.

This research on early polynesians was found on Maui inside Haleakala in connection with a burial there, which was carbon dated between 600 and 700 A.D. Earlier settlements found were on Hawaii, Moloka'i and Oahu. These first Polynesians basically lived close to the shore, built no heiau, did very little agricultural work, and existed mainly on ocean products and birds. We do know they ate much of Hawaii's early unique bird population to extinction.

Later, around 1000 to 1100 A.D. these people were overrun by a highly organized migrating group from the Marquesas and Society Islands. Then sometime after the mid 1500s the Spanish arrived, (possibly three different times). You are entitled to raise your eyebrows at this Spanish news, especially if you are from a country who feels your ancestors did all the important exploring in early times. But the

Hawaiians have no doubt that the Spanish were the first white people here. What the Spaniards did here is recorded in Hawaiian oral history. Modern literary scholars have also come up with lots of proof, and now it's up to you to accept, or reject it.

Maui has been less intensively studied by archaeologists and anthropologists compared to Oahu, Moloka'i, and Hawaii. Even research such as the one in Haleakala in 1920 has not been completed or published. A few leeward shoreside sites have been studied that were occupied in the 1500s and 1600s, but in large measure, scholars still have not unraveled the sequence of economic, social, and political change that led to the development of the powerful Maui chiefdoms as witnessed by Captain James Cook and others.

GEOLOGY

You might also like to know that the summit of this volcano was originally 3,000 feet higher than it is today. The whole island of Maui was way up there a million years ago. It has since sunk 3,500 feet into the mantle of the earth, and is still sinking as it moves northwest on the Pacific tectonic plate. In fact, Maui only has about four million years of life left before it becomes an atoll about to disappear under the ocean.

Originally Maui was part of a much larger island which geologists have named Maui Nui, or Greater Maui. This island once consisted of Maui, Kaho'olawe, Lana'i, and Moloka'i. A rise of a few hundred feet in the ocean after former ice ages helped to separate these islands. The fact that Maui Nui

sank, made the islands as you see them today.
Erosion from the top down does little in reducing the
height and size of any Hawaiian Island. Sinking is
what does most of it, along with the sides of volcanoes
sliding into the ocean. The islands are sinking at the
same rate that your fingernails grow. Someday the
ocean will flood across Maui's central isthmus and we
will have two islands. But don't get shook up and sell
that condo unit in Kihei, the separation won't happen
for another 50,000 years. The warning is already out
that the low land area prone to swamping along the
Kihei shore will see an increase in ocean flooding in
the very near future. By the time the ocean has cut
off East and West Maui we will have the ninth
Hawaiian Island, Loihi, which is now building up
from the ocean floor to the south of The Big Island.
And then by the time that island is inhabitated, there
will be another island growing from the ocean floor.
And so it will go, on and on.

According to research, Haleakala's summit
depression is from 2,000 to 2,500 feet deep, 21 miles
in circumference, seven miles long by two miles wide.
The tallest cinder cone on the floor is about 600 feet
high. What you gaze into is not a crater or a caldera.
(A crater is less than one mile in diameter, and a
caldera is more than a mile in diameter). It is a
depression caused by erosion. A later eruption of
cinder cones happened on its floor.

This mountain is often called "the largest
extinct volcanic crater in the world," and "a dormant
volcano."

False in both respects.

Haleakala is still active according to volcano
scientists. Twenty eruptions have happened in the
last 2,500 years in the summit basin alone, and it is

likely that some of this action was witnessed by Hawaiians. The southwest rift zone has erupted at least five times in the last 900 years. In geological time, this is just a blink of an eye. Researchers fully expect Haleakala to erupt again someday. But like archeological surveys on Maui, the island also has been short-changed in volcano studies. Over the next few years scientists at the U.S. Geological Survey's Hawaiian Volcano Observatory will be expanding their studies of Haleakala. Perhaps then we will know when the next Big Show might be.

As for large extinct volcanic craters, you should visit Africa where one crater is larger than Oahu.

***

Adjacent to Haleakala's summit is Science City. The first precise instrument measurements showing the Pacific Plate moving northwest at about four inches a year, carrying the Hawaiian Islands along with it, were taken here. The buildings are also home to lunar and solar observations, a satellite tracking station, and a radio and TV repeater station. When a winter storm thrashes around the summit with ice and snow driven by 100 mile-an-hour winds, and all television service goes out on Moloka'i, Lana'i, Maui and The Big Island, this city gets all the blame (which they don't deserve). But then, we are about to put an automobile on Mars, so why can't science operate through a little snow and ice on earth?

The business of astronomy atop this volcano is due to expand in the coming years with medium-size telescopes.

ONWARD TO HANA

Driving the road to Hana, and beyond to
Kipahulu, will easily take all day. Perhaps two days,
staying overnight in Hana. Today this route is touted
as "the most scenic drive in Hawaii." That's a fair
statement, only it gained that reputation after the old
road from Hilo to Waimea on the Big Island was
bypassed by a new highway in the 1950s.

I made the Hana trip in 1935 when the
unpaved road was first opened to vehicular traffic. I
became car sick for the first and last time in my life.
My father had to stop six times while I threw up
alongside the road. Don't laugh. I know of two
touring companies who recently gave up offering the
Hana trip because customers in the rear seats often
got car sick.

Pick up any photographic book or magazine on
Maui today, and what you get is a perfect lecture on
"Save What's Left of the Beauty and Uniqueness of
this Island." Most of this plea is directed at the
country serviced by the Hana road.

The undisputed king of such books is Robert
Wenkam with his two volumes, *Maui, The Last*

Hawaiian Place, 1970, and *Maui No Ka Oi*, 1980. These coffee table type books are treasures and should be kept in print. Wenkam's summary of this road is, "The Hana Road is not a road to go anywhere on - the Hana Road is a destination in itself."

In my estimation, the scenic road begins at a place called Huelo, about 14 miles out of Kahului. But general visitor information has it beginning with the town of Pa'ia. We'll begin there.

PAIA

Paia was, and in some respects still is, the icon of the typical island country town born of sugar production in the 1800s and having to weather the 20th century. And like almost every mining or cattle town in the American west, it mostly burned down in 1930. Then it was dealt a double whammy in 1946 when a tsunami swept the area. Each time, stores were rebuilt and commerce continued, only today it no longer services plantation residents, but tourists. Therefore, a bank has become an art gallery, a grocery store a pizza and food parlor, a pool hall a beach wear outlet. Athletic young men and women, their thin bodies (many sporting tattoos) the result of a vegetarian diet, walk the streets with surfboards headed for the beach. The town jumps to the windsurfers and euro-youth beat. Visitors pause to browse the shops, have a cold drink, and buy a sandwich for the Hana trip.

Up the road a mile is Ho'okipa Beach Park, surely the most popular park in Maui County. Water activity is on a schedule. From dawn to noon traditional surfers are out on their surf boards at both ends of the park. Come noon the trade wind traditionally picks up and surf-sailing takes over the Kahului end of the park. Sightseers line the hillsides overlooking the beach as photographers train telescopic lenses on the action. And action it is! Multi-colored butterfly sails go zipping over blue water far out toward the horizon, then turn and cruise toward shore to occasionally catch a wave. Day after day I sat there hoping to get THE picture. Day after day the photo turned out the same -- okay, but not as spectacular as I saw it in my mind's eye. Hint: the best action is between 2 and 4 p.m. Saturday, Sunday, or any holiday.

***

The Hana highway and its scenery for the next three miles is not impressive. However, you are introduced to guava. Miles of it, with pulpy fruit in season falling onto the highway and smelling of -- well -- guava. On Oahu or the Big Island, pickup trucks line the shoulder of the road while families load up on the fruit. Juice and jam and jelly businesses pay good money for it. Apparently this is not so on Maui. Did you know that there is so much vitamin C in guava that four ounces of the fruit will protect an arctic explorer from scurvy for three months? And that during World War II troops in the Pacific were suppled with its products to build up their resistance against infection? Go eat a guava.

Along this section of the Hana drive is a sightseeing spot called Twin Falls. This is all I'm gonna tell you about it. I wouldn't stop here on a bet as the chances are my car will be vandalized. Local residents have a comment about this place. "A police sub-station should be built there," they say.

There is no point in taking the Huelo road toward the ocean. Kaulanapueo church established in 1853 offers nothing exciting, and you don't get near the ocean. Only if you came this way 70 years ago would you see a difference. Back then people lived in the broad gulches on either side of Hueo ridge where they maintained taro and banana patches. Today, houses are perched on the ridge to take advantage of any view and to have pasture for a horse or cattle. The gulches have since reverted to jungle.

From here on is where today's residents of Maui consider the Hana road really starts. It's also where the pesky bamboo begins to cover entire mountainsides. Bamboos are a shrub or tree, not a grass, although in a very broad sense they belong to the grass family. They can grow to be more than 100 feet tall. There is useless, ornamental and timber bamboo. No botanist tells you what type of bamboo covers this mountainside, except to say it is green bamboo, so I'll tell you about it.

INTRODUCING MAUI

Back in the early days when the first Polynesians came to Hawaii in double canoes from the Society Islands, they brought plants they treasured for everyday existence. One of the earliest canoes brought Mr. and Mrs. Demigod Q. Maui. After beaching their canoe, Mrs. Maui began unpacking.

Suddenly she confronted her husband. "I see you brought the breadfruit slips from grandmother's yard."

"Yep," he said.

"You didn't forget the taro."

61

"I didn't forget," he said, squaring his shoulders with pride.

"And I'm glad you brought both a male and female chicken and pig,"

"I made sure of that," he said with a smug smile.

Then Mrs. Maui opened the package of bamboo shoots. "What is this?" she cried. "You got the wrong bamboo."

"I didn't know what kind to bring," he explained. "I just picked the first one I could find."

"Stupid! This is useless bamboo. Utterly worthless. We can't build our house with this like we did back home. We can't weave it. Now we have to make our houses out of *pili* grass and *ti* leaves. Why, the young shoots of this bamboo don't even taste good."

Maui hung his head in shame as his wife continued to mumble. "So stupid. The next thing I know, you will probably take your fishing net and go climb this volcano to catch the sun."

A light went off in Maui's head, and his face shone with a holy glow. "I could do that you know," he cried. "That would make the sun slow down in going across the heavens, and give you more time to dry your *kapa*. Will you forgive me then?"

Mrs. Maui threw the bundle of bamboo shoots at her husband. "Here, on your way to the sunrise, go plant this stuff on the mountainside. It might make the place look pretty in about 2,000 years."

So help me! That's how Maui came to snare the sun, and that's the useless bamboo along the Hana Road. I've got to admit, it's pretty.

***

I apologize for using the demigod Maui in this

humorous fashion. But the truth is that I don't dare connect the legendary Maui with the island Maui in a serious manner because of a lecture I received about a half century ago. My professor was Bengt Danielson, the leading anthropologist in the South Pacific. He set me straight on Maui during a visit to the Tuamoto cluster of islands between Tahiti and the Marquesas.

According to this researcher, Maui came into Polynesian life long before the first human set foot on Hawaii. He evolved somewhere, on some island, between Tahiti and New Zealand before the birth of Christ. Therefore, the Maui of Maui snaring the sun at Haleakala, and hooking up the Hawaiian archipelago from the bottom of the ocean is a copy retold to suit Hawaii.

In Polynesian lore, Maui appeared long after the earth, sea, sky and man were created. He figured the days were too short and the nights too long, so he paddled his canoe to the horizon and snared the sun as it was setting over the edge of the ocean. He set the sun free only after it promised to move more slowly across the heavens.

Maui also created the first dog, and gave fire to his people.

But his greatest deed was to snag his fish hook on the bottom of the ocean and pull up islands for the Polynesians to settle. High volcanic "high" islands like those of Hawaii, Tahiti and the Marquesas were not fished up by Maui. These islands were creations of the fire goddess Pele. The islands Maui snagged were atolls as in all the Tuamotu islands. These were coral reef islands with protected lagoons for fishing.

Briefly, that's the story of Maui, and no Polynesian south of Hawaii will let me forget it.

MOVING ALONG

Beside the road you will begin to see sections of a water ditch system that runs from Hana toward the central isthmus. There are four ditch systems. The other ones are higher on the volcano, deeper into the jungle. Construction of these ditches around 1882 and the transportation afterward of untold billions of gallons in them made central and west Maui what they are today. People are discouraged from walking the upper ditch trails as a hiking experience. Hikers need permission from the Division of State Forestry, and to have a stool sample analyzed by the Board of Health before they go.

One of the things that probably enticed you to take this Hana drive is scenes of waterfalls splashing into pools ringed by ferns and flowering plants. Every photograph includes one or more lovelies with or without skimpy bathing suits and flowers in their dark hair. These waterfall pools are located in five places at the head of gulches along this route. The road has been widened to accept maybe four or five cars near such curves. You should know that those photos are taken only at special times of the year when rainfall feeds the waterfalls and flowers are around. Chances are excellent the scene will be somewhat disappointing to the average visitor because the weather will not be accommodating. Still, it's worth a stop and a swim.

The first real get-out-of-your-car-and-stretch-your-legs-stop is Waikamoi Ridge nature walk. The trails are well maintained, but not one plant or tree is signed as to what it is. So you walk blind and ignorant in the greenery, unless you have the guide book *Maui's Hana Highway* by Angela Kay Kepler. And even then, some visitors complain that the author doesn't give enough information.

Once while walking, I came across a tour group standing waist-deep in the bushes. A guide was urging them to chew certain leaves. She had names of flowers and trees rolling off her tongue along with their origin and what they were used for yesterday and today. I couldn't help but include myself in this group. This walk suddenly became exciting and educational.

Toward the end of the tour, I asked the guide, "Is this a County or State Park?"

"State," she said.

"You would think they would identify the plants for the enjoyment of the average visitor."

"They don't. It's that way in all their botanical parks."

"Why don't they do it? No money? Manpower?"

She shrugged. "That's Hawaii."

***

If you started your tour of the Hana Road before 10:30 a.m., you are the lucky one. At 10:31 the traffic doubles going toward Hana. The turn-around to Kahalui begins at 2 p.m. and doubles at 3:46 as visitors rush to get back to their condo for a shower, a drink and dinner. Set your watch.

. "That's Hawaii," also extends itself to the Ke'anae Arboretum. Labeling of some trees and bushes was attempted long ago, but some of the identifications are comical today. A tree with identification is no longer there, while another example of it is elsewhere. No one moved the sign.

One scene in this park gives a history lesson if

you understand your Hawaiiana. Deep into the park are several taro patches being fed by the time-honored *awai* (water ditch). Whoever laid out, or restored those patches did it right. The typical Hawaiian taro patch was not a simple area of mud holding taro plants. It was a complex system. Ringing the patch was sugar cane, bananas and *ti*, (a leafy plant known as Cordyline in the rest of the tropical world) all staples for everyday use by a native household. The sweet potato patch to one side is also tradition. Such a complex is in this park.

THE GREENING OF MAUI

By now you have read accounts of how some botanists say the greening of Maui took thousands, if not a million years to accomplish. That over a long, long time, one by one, spores and seeds of plants, and insects and birds used the ocean, or the air, to travel thousands of miles across the Pacific to populate Maui. The popular saying is, "new species arrived on Maui at the rate of one every 40,000 years."

Hogwash! That old research was thrown out with the dishwater long ago.

All the basic stuff that greened Maui in the very beginning was already here. It was sitting right next door on another island only a few miles across the ocean. Maui's lavas just had to cool enough to let plants, insects and birds gain a foothold. Maui got its dressing from Oahu; which in turn got its greenery from Kauai; which got its from a huge island that today has sunk leaving single rocks or reefs known as Nihoa and Necker Islands, and Kure Atoll and Midway Islands; and their plant, insect and bird life came from islands that are the Emperor Seamounts long gone underwater.

This process of greening-up an island is called "Island Hopping." It's a quick trick for plants, seeds and land birds to hop over a few miles of ocean. This also applies to smaller fish and reef life that migrated from island to island.

Or as H.W. Menard, one of the world's foremost marine geologists said in his book *Islands*, the bible of modern island geology, "The very concept of sequential development of islands that drift away from a hot spot has the corollary that plants and animals can migrate counter to island drift. If botanists believe that Hawaiian plants are much older than the islands, why not? Certain plants, animals and marine life have been migrating along the Hawaiian archipelago for all of Tertiary time."

Also, please don't think that it takes thousands upon thousands of years for a different species to evolve from original parents. Different species can evolve within a few hundred years. It all depends on how many generations there are in a year. This happens quickly in Hawaiian moths, forest flies and tree snails.

Once the initial greening of Maui had been accomplished, other plants were added as new species arrived by bird droppings, by flotsam, or by air which is thick with life.

How thick is the air over Maui? Let's make believe that Haleakala erupted last month and covered the island with a dense layer of lava and ash so that no living thing existed on Maui. As soon as the ash cooled enough to support life (probably within a month or two) and a heavy rain occured, the ash would be covered with new life just bursting to grow as more rain falls. The more rain, the quicker it will happen. This process goes on all the time on The Big Island. Visitors who witnessed the 1960 eruption in Puna that covered Kapoho Village, return today and are amazed that a forest of ironwoods 30 feet tall covers the area.

I have seen Maui's air heavy with life. Forty years ago I rode in a light airplane with a botanist who dragged a fine-mesh parachute behind the plane. He started the experiment 60 miles out at sea off windward Maui and the Big Island. You simply would not believe the vast amount of life there was in that net! Everything from microscopic spores of ferns to winged seeds to spiders. All would have been dumped onto Maui's volcanic ash with the first rainfall coming in from windward, and the greening and repopulation of Maui would show within a year.

KE'ANAE

Now comes Ke'anae peninsula, an experience to raise bumps on your skin, or as they say in Hawaii, "chicken skin." This area has a scenic waterfront, a church, and many taro patches. A beautiful place to have a picnic. Again, you have to know your history to appreciate some things. During the 1800s and up to the mid-1900s, all such populated remote communities were serviced by boat. You can find evidence of this by searching the coastline to discover where the ship would anchor offshore and send a launch ashore with cargo. Tidal waves have long destroyed some of the evidence, but you can still find sections of the concrete wharf and mooring posts.

Lanakila Church (1860) is picturesque with its

rough stone walls. The door is always open, and a coconut is usually the door stop. Red and green *ti* frame the ancient windows.

Unpaved driveways lead deeper into the peninsula toward the taro patches. Along one road is an answer as to why I treasure Maui. I always thrill when visiting several graves bordering this particular taro patch. I'm a graveyard buff. I love to read headstones. So and So, born and the date, died and the date. All over Hawaii the graves are like that. Even the old Hawaiian ones. Of course, the wording on most graves is due to Christian influence.

But here among the taro patches are two Hawaiian graves where legend flies in the face of the missionaries. I can just hear the Hawaiian saying, "When I die, I want to die a Hawaiian. Do my headstone in Hawaiian."

> And so we have two brothers:
> Joseph A. Halemano
> *Hanau* July 4, 1878
> *Make* June 12, 1904
>
> David Halemano
> *Hanau* Jan. 25, 1880
> *Make* Sept. 2, 1883

ONWARD

Few visitors venture into Wailua Valley. The only thing that might lure them is the history of St. Gavriel's mission. The story goes that the people needed coral blocks and sand to finish the building. A sudden storm heaped the needed materials on a nearby shore in a single night. The builders used what they needed, and a short time later another storm washed away the remaining material.

Pua'aka'a Wayside provides a handy restroom stop. It also offers a picnic area, waterfall, and pool. Compared to years ago, toilet facilities have gotten better and better, while park improvements have gone downhill. The park looks and feels trashy.

***

The road to the ocean in the Nahiku district is obvious, but unsigned. Several tour booklets say the trip is not worth taking. Well, that's all in the eye and mind of the writer. Something happened to me here a quarter of a century ago that had a profound effect on my favorite pastime - flower gardening.

They say this is the wettest spot on Maui. (But they also say the Kahakuloa area in the West Maui mountains is the wettest spot, so who knows.) The rainfall at Nahiku was so plentiful that a rubber plantation, the first in the U.S., was started in one part of this district in 1905. Nine hundred acres of the trees were planted. But by 1916 the plantation folded due to the high cost of getting the sap out of the trees and shipping it to be processed.

It was while I was searching for a surviving rubber tree that a surprising event occured in the forest.

As you can see, the common yellow and white ginger crowd the sides of the road and wander into the jungle. You also may have noticed that the two grow side by side in fields of their own, but never mingle in the same patch. The yellow ginger grows taller, the white smaller. The yellow ginger flower is a butter yellow with a brighter yellow center. The white has a lime green center. Both have the same perfume, although the scent of the white appears richer.

Imagine my surprise when I came upon a ginger flower that was half bright yellow and half white. What was this? How did it happen? Was it cross pollination, or did the roots somehow mate?

This crisscross was unknown for this plant in the science of botany. When I told people about it, they laughed.

I took a piece of root home to my garden at Volcano on the Big Island. When I had a large enough patch, I gave roots to the State Forestry Department, and they planted it along the botanical walk at Akaka Falls near Hilo. Now collectors from all over visit me asking for a root. To this day, no one has explained how this cross happened to this flower. I have named the flower the "Gold Strike Ginger."

You also may have noticed a red *ti* leaf along this Hana drive. The green *ti* is the common native variety, very useful yesterday and today in Hawaiian culture. The plant is known as the Cordyline in the rest of the tropical world. It comes in half a hundred leaf patterns in a mixture of colors. The red *ti* seems to be the pride of Hana as it flourishes here, but it's scarcely seen elsewhere on Maui. One of the biggest patches of this red *ti* borders one home along this road.

***

The road ends seaside at a place called Honolulu. It is not known if this place was named after our capitol city on Oahu, but it isn't likely. They say Honolulu means "sheltered harbor." Well, maybe. But Honolulu was the name of a prominent rock that was beside Nuuanu stream long before the name became connected with that harbor. (The harbor was called Kou).

Honolulu also means a quiet ocean area in a place where chiefs gather to hold a ceremony. This fits the atmosphere you experience at the end of this road. No place could be more suitable for a picnic. Also check out the small waterfall issuing from rocks like an artesian spring and filling a shore-side pool. Here's that place for a private photo in a natural setting, rain or no rain.

***

The Hana road now begins to traverse more open country as it gradually goes downhill toward Hana Airport. The bad curves are being widened here and there by the State. It was one of these curves that did in one of the pickup campers my family rented to travelers back in the 1960s. A renter took a curve badly early one Sunday morning, and the unit tipped on its side in the guava bushes. No one was hurt. The driver walked for miles until he came to a house with a telephone. He called the rental station in Kahului, where someone called the Hana police and the head office in Hilo on Hawaii Island. It had long been proven that the camper rental staff in Hilo could handle a situation in Hana quicker than those in Kahului, given the nature of the Hana Road at that time.

The Hilo office used a Cessna with my son as pilot. He and I flew into the Hana airport and walked to the accident site. We were at the scene before the

Hana police arrived.

For visitors who have never been to Tahiti, let me say that the general scenery from the Hana Airport into Hana comes the closest to resembling rural Tahiti. (Only one other place in Hawaii, a mile-long stretch on the lower Puna coast, has a simular look.) The combination of old stone walls, coconut trees, and especially breadfruit, gives this area the Tahitian flavor.

Wai'anapanapa State Park offers a good example of a black sand beach. It holds the area's only public campground and 12 overnight housekeeping cabins on 120 acres. It takes a year in advance to reserve a cabin here - believe me.

HANA

And now Hana. There is so much to say about this district, and so much that has been said and written, that I'm inclined to give you just an overview.

One of the early westerners to survey this area was August Unna, a Dane who started the first sugar plantation here in 1851. His comment is valid today, "Plenty of good soil, rain and sunshine continually blending and interchanging, and the country is covered at all times with luxuriant verdure."

In 1890, *kapa* (cloth beaten from tree bark) was still made and worn here. Even during the first half of this century, Hana was known as "a remote and fully Hawaiian district." Today, artists, song writers and authors find it "a power spot that sends the spirit on creative adventures."

Island historian Ruth Tabrah observes that the effect of tourism on Hana has been to mellow visitors and new residents into being as Hawaiian as the Hawaiians they meet there.

While viewing Hana harbor, it helps to know that this one bay has probably seen more fleets of Hawaiian battle canoes come and go than any other

74

landing site on Maui, as Hana was the "seat of power" in the old days. Families of ancient Hawaiian families of high blood lines who ruled different islands in the past had their roots here. It was also the closest landfall to the Big Island where most of the invasions originated. Umi, a great king of Hawaii Island, erected an image of a warrior on the high point beside the entrance to this bay. The rock was given the name Pu'u Kii, or Hill of an Image. Much later, bonfires were kept burning at night atop the hill to guide fishermen back home after dark. (The only other known point of land to have this signal was on south/eastern Moloka'i on land that became my family's homestead in the 1920s.) A lightmast was erected here in 1908.

Milestones for change in Hana started with the first Christian church in 1838. This made the most profound personal impact on the residents. Sugar plantation operations in the mid-1800s also changed their lifestyle. The plantation evolved into a cattle ranch in 1945, and then moved into tourism. But even with the crush of visitors, the centerpiece of the district is the Hasegawa General Store, a family concern that is part museum, part store, part everything. I can remember the store as a child when I watched my parents buy *lauhala* matting here for our floors. That tells you how long ago that was. Today the largest *lauhala* items you can buy anywhere in Hawaii are table place mats or hats.

All over Hawaii the art of *lauhala* matting for floors has disappeared. (Samoa became the source for this in the 1950's.) It has been 60 years since I've seen a traditional Hana white *lauhala* mat made with polished bamboo strips running through it, and maidenhair fern woven into its corners.

KIPAHULU

While many visitors turn around in Hana and
head back the way they came, more and more are
continuing to Kipahulu - and still onward around the
eastern end of the island back to central Maui via
Ulupalakua. What they find in the road to Kipahulu
is more of the Hana Road, although not as cliffy or
tricky at the curves.

Kipahulu, along with the summit swamp of
Waialeale on Kauai, the bogs of Moloka'i and west
Maui mountain ridges, is considered one of the last
true wilderness areas in all Hawaii. The upland
district is almost completely free of introduced plants.
Several endangered Hawaii birds exist here.

My image of Kipahulu comes from two
adventures. The first was a phone call from one of
our motorhome renters who stayed overnight in the
National Park campground at Seven Sacred Pools.
The driver was standing on the bridge overlooking the
pools when he inadvertantly dropped the motorhome
keys in the water.

Our client was locked out of his mobile home.
He went to a private home and called the office at

Kahului to ask for a spare set of keys. The Maui office called the head office in Hilo. Within minutes we were in the Cessna heading for east Maui with a spare set of keys. We made a couple of passes over the campground while I tied the keys to a handkerchief, then parachuted them to the waving driver. Problem solved in less than an hour in far-out Kipahulu. I wonder if any car rental company today handles emergencies in such an imaginative fashion?

There is no such thing as seven sacred pools as some tourist literature would have you believe. I know. I know. You've stood on the bridge, or at the bottom of the stream, and tried to count the pools. Everyone does it. The name is pure advertising for the tourist trade. See the scene as the cascading waterfalls of Ohe'o stream which is excitingly beautiful with far more than seven smallish waterfalls and cascades.

***

Back in the decade of the 1950s we lived on Windward Oahu. Our neighbor was Tap Pryor who masterminded and produced the Oahu oceanarium Sea Life Park. He had been a Marine helicopter pilot, and flying around Maui one day he was struck by the beauty of the Kipahulu district. He told his father Sam Pryor, who was executive vice president of Pan American Airways, about this paradise. So in retirement Sam bought some acreage at Kipahulu. The paved road around this part of Maui ended at his gate.

My wife Joann had a side business of building vacation houses along with her architectural Scale Model business. She was the first licensed woman contractor in Hawaii. Her speciality was A-frames, using cedar from western Canada. Tap Pryor asked her to build a shoreside cottage on his father's property so they could begin spending time there and dream of the future. She did.

The one-bedroom cottage was successful, and the architecture fit in so well with the Kipahulu landscape that Sam abandoned his architectural plans to build a grand house, and asked her to build a three-bedroom A frame with extensive decks overlooking a waterfall, the ocean and mountains. There was also to be a separate A-frame garage with guest quarters, and a gazebo overlooking a gulch with waterfall.

These projects took the better part of six months to build, and we lived on Maui while they were accomplished. The lumber used was prime stuff specially cut to lengths for the towering A-frame roof and floor joists. A trucker had never moved such wood to Hana and Kipahulu before (prior to this, building materials were usually brought in by boat), and the curves with narrow bridges at the head of the gulches became a problem. Please note as you drive the Hana road that the concrete bridges are somewhat battered and nicked at the ends. We didn't do all of that, but Sam Pryor's lumber did some of the damage.

Soon after Sam moved in, his friend Charles Lindbergh decided to retire in Kipahulu. He asked Sam to sell him a few acres. Lindbergh bought it with dolls. Both Pryor and Lindbergh were doll collectors, with Sam's collection the larger one as every Pan American pilot flying the world was on the lookout for a unique doll to bring back to their boss. So in lieu of cash, Charles gave Sam his doll collection for the property.

It is also interesting that Sam Pryor's uncle, who was a banker in St. Louis, loaned Lindbergh the $15,000 necessary for him to buy the Spirit of St. Louis to fly the Atlantic. After that, Lindbergh's life was more or less tied up with Pan American Airways, and then Kipahulu, so it is no coincidence that both men are buried in the same plot there. They planned it that way.

Sam Pryor restored the old Congregational Church nearby, and with the help of the people of Kipahulu, furnished as it was originally. People who had the old pews in their homes brought them back. Pryor found an ancient organ in New Hampshire, and had copies of the original church chandeliers made in Connecticut. The church held its first service in 20 years on Thanksgiving Day, 1965. It goes without saying that the public should treat this church and its graveyard with the reverence it deserves when visiting the site.

AROUND THE BACK SIDE

The rest of the way around eastern Maui back to the central isthmus takes a little doing as about six miles of the road is unpaved. This stretch warrants a warning: "Road subject to severe erosion and flooding during rains."

The first real stop along the way is Huialoha Church (1859) situated on a picturesque peninsula. The road to it has no sign. I once cooked dinner for the entire congregation in appreciation for a historic Hawaiian-type service, and permission to sleep in the church overnight as our group walking around Maui in 1975 were camping out and the weather was bad. (The menu was chopped steak and onions with carrot and raisin salad, and chocolate cake with coconut frosting). There is an interesting graveyard. The ruins of an old rock school house next to the ocean is the subject of the cover of this book.

A mile further on is Kaupo Gulch with its lone store built in 1925. The owner was Nick Soon, a Chinese merchant who spoke Hawaiian and owned a string of stores around east Maui. Early in 1970 he retired, but not before making me promise to visit his many cousins who also owned stores in Tahiti and neighboring Society Islands. I have traveled enough throughout the Pacific to know that any out-of-the-way country store you enter, you will find a Chinese merchant. He will sell you everything you have no use for. I went to Moorea where Soon's cousin sold me a Coleman lantern that worked on gin. Now it is disappointing to enter this Kaupo store to find a pretty Caucasian lady as proprietor. She sold me ice cream and a cold drink. But as time goes on, perhaps she will make her own history at Kaupo Store.

You might wave as you pass St. Joseph's Church (1861).

From here on there is fantastic scenery oceanside and mountainside even though the area at this lower altitude will usually be dry. The highlands have views of deep gulches and waterfalls.

After Kaupo Gulch, the high pastures will glow an emerald green, and you can just imagine the cattle growing fatter by the hour. The blue/blue ocean offshore will usually be streaked with white caps caused by a brisk trade wind blowing down the channel between Maui and the Big Island. Mauna Kea and Mauna Loa volcanoes show purple in the distance.

The road dips down to the shore at a place called Manalu Bay. The waterfront is interesting because it's paved with water-worn rocks that range in size from tennis balls to bowling balls to wrecking balls. Instead of just looking, sit and listen. The rocks roll in the surf producing a thunder.

***

Maui's shape is not unique in this world. It

has a clone in size and shape in the Pacific. Tahiti also has a large bulbous main island and an isthmus connecting a smaller knob of island. This likeness to Maui was recognized early when Polynesians migrated from Tahiti. They even named the district you now are traveling through Kahikinui, which is the name for the larger portion of Tahiti. This section faces Tahiti which lies 2,400 miles beyond the horizon.

It is truly hard to visualize that this leeward side of Maui once had a large resident population of Hawaiians who fished and planted crops along these slopes in the 1600s. One hundred and fifty years of running cattle has drastically altered the landscape. It all looks so dry, treeless and hopeless for any modern agricultural enterprise. Yet, there are plans to make this area into farm lots by the Hawaiian Homes Department. They plan to replant the slopes with koa, ohia and other native forest trees to again increase the rainfall. Hawaiian homesteaders will plant crops, raise animals and live here along the lines of the plan for central Moloka'i in the early 1920s.

Now it's gradually all uphill on pavement that is never renewed, but adequately patched. The major tree on the landscape is the *wiliwili* which produces red, orange, or yellowish beans that can be made into jewelry. A long time ago someone planted yellow Mexican poppies along the road. They still bloom seasonally. Each time I come this way, I harvest seeds to plant these poppies in my garden.

***

Along the shore is the King's Trail or jeep road that I wrote about starting at La Perouse Bay. Kings in the distant past may have ordered the route built and maintained, but no king would have been caught dead walking that trail in the old days. Hawaiian ruling chiefs did very little long-distance walking. They journeyed in canoes. But after the horse was introduced in the early 1800s, trails such as this one had to be improved, and Kings Kamehameha III, IV and V did order upgrades to certain foot trails around the island using convict labor. The trail today is a very bad four-wheel-drive path.

In our 1975 walk around historic Maui, 10 of us braved that trail, and slept alongside it one night. That night started out as one of the worst events of my life. The most numerous inhabitant of the lava shore-side landscape was (and still is) centipedes. There were millions of them. There was no chance to lie down on our sleeping bags until one of us discovered an empty concrete cattle drinking trough. The coffin-like watering trough was about 20-feet long by three feet wide, by three feet deep. After spraying the entire outside with Raid, we slept inside the trough head to foot.

ULUPALAKUA

Finally, travelers gain enough altitude to reach an area where rainfall is adequate for lush growth. This is the world of Ulupalakua. If this ranch property were ever subdivided and sold, and a highway built linking Wailea and Kihei at the shore, this area would be absolute heaven for living. Look around you! There's deep soil, adequate rainfall and the right mixture of the tropics and coolness to grow almost anything. Pastures with grass satisfy any animal. Scenery spans five Hawaiian islands with sunset extravaganzas. My goodness, what more could a person want!

Several men also thought that over the past 150 years, and they made, (and kept to themselves) what you see today.

First in 1840 was a sugar man who also grew potatoes for the California gold rush. His sugar mill is still here, very picturesque, but difficult to approach without permission.

Then came a Honolulu businessman who imported cattle, planted most of the trees you see here today, built a New England - style mansion, and created a social atmosphere that attracted Hawaiian kings and the rich and famous. The original pink rose that became the flower of Maui was his import.

The Baldwin family took over Ulupalakua after the turn of the century and consolidated neighboring ranches to make this the largest cattle operation on Maui. Today, grapes is a visible industry for the visitor in this area.

***

The highway dips and rolls back to the Kula district. But there is one last stop that calls for your camera. About a mile out of the Ulupalakua ranch store, the road widens on the ocean side overlooking a pasture that slopes down to Kihei. This is the scenic stop to end all scenic stops. The panoramic view on the left is of the Big Island, Kaho'olawe, Lana'i, the entire south Maui coast, a good chunk of west Maui, to a piece of Moloka'i. I don't know of any single scene in all Hawaii that can beat this on a clear evening when the sun is setting over Lana'i.

ARE WE THERE YET?

So, how do I end this book?

With a story, of course.

Back we go to Kipahulu and Sam Pryor. Sam ended his days making his estate a forest of tropical plants and flowers. He loved animals and raised gibbons. One of the gibbons took a shine to Joann and would not leave her side whenever we visited.

One year we were invited to Sam's birthday party along with other special guests from Hawaii and the Mainland. Joann spent all morning in a Kahului beauty shop getting her hair done before we motored to Kipahulu.

Cocktails were served on the spacious deck that was specially built to be like the prow of a ship overlooking the ocean. When Joann sat, her friend the gibbon was right with her. After the normal introduction of petting and pawing, the gibbon took up a position behind her and began inspecting her hair. He pawed her scalp hair by hair looking for you-know-what.

Sam and his wife were apologetic, and wanted to cage the gibbon.

"Don't be silly," said Joann. "He's doing what comes naturally. I don't mind."

The guests were enthralled.

But every so often Joann would lean over and whisper to me, "Is he finding anything? Is he putting his fingers into his mouth?"

***

That's it. Go enjoy Maui.

MAUI INFORMATION

All books are available at local bookstores.

Haleakala: A Guide to the Mountain, Cameron B and Angela Kay Kepler, Mutual Publishing, Honolulu, Hi 1988;

Lahaina, Royal Capital of Hawaii, Roy Nickerson, Hawaiian Service, Honolulu, Hi 1978.

Maui's Hana Highway, A Visitor's Guide, Angela Kay Kepler, Mutual Publishing, Honolulu, Hi 1995.

Maui Remembers - A Local History, Gail Bartholomew and Bren Bailey, Mutual Publishing, Honolulu, Hi 1994.

Mowee, An Informal History of The Hawaiian Island, Cummins E. Speakman, Jr. Peabody Museum of Salem, Salem, Mass 1978.

*On The Hama Coast,*Emphasis International Ltd. Hong Kong, 1992.

Roadside Geology of Hawaii, Richard W. Hazlett
and Donald W. Hyndman, Mountain Press
Publishing, 1996.

*Sunny South Maui, A guide to Kihei, Wailea &
Makena, Including Kahoolawe*, Angela Kay Kepler,
Mutual Publishing, Honolulu, Hi 1992.

The Narrow Winding Road, Shave Ice Solomon,
T-N Productions, Hana, Maui, 1994.

OTHER TOUR BOOKS BY GORDON MORSE

My Moloka'i, My Island Publishing, Volcano, Hi
1991.

My Owhyhee, My Island Publishing, Volcano, Hi
1992.

Summit and Oceanfront Tour of Kilauea Volcano,
My Island Publishing, Volcano, Hi 1996.